THESE WORDS: WEDDINGS AND AFTER

WEDDINGS AND AFTER

AN ESSAY AND POETRY
BY
WILLIAM McILVANNEY

MAINSTREAM
PUBLISHING·EDINBURGH

A

First published in 1984 by
MAINSTREAM PUBLISHING,
7 Albany Street, Edinburgh, EH1 3UG.

00021 5249

The publisher acknowledges financial assistance from the
Scottish Arts Council in the publication of this volume.

ISBN 0 906391 61 X

Typeset 11/13 point Garamond by Studioscope
in conjunction with Mainstream Publishing.

Printed in Great Britain by
Forsyth Middleton & Co. Ltd., Kilsyth.

Contents

Also by William McIlvanney
Docherty
Remedy is None
A Gift from Nessus
Laidlaw
The Papers of Tony Veitch

Poetry
The Longships in Harbour

To the friends of 'The Admiral'.

Making these words—

The children, callipered with love, are hobbling still.
The wise men at their games are splitting stars.
The thinkers immolate, the senses cower,
The nipple welters blood.

For madness a made craft:
My hand writes 'water' on the burning paper.

'The Sacred Wood' Revisited:
An Essay

THE following is a response to re-reading *The Sacred Wood* by
T. S. Eliot. The book was written a long time ago (First Edition,
1920) and I should perhaps explain why it seems important to me
to re-examine it and why it seems relevant to offer that re-
examination preceding a book of poetry being published more than
sixty years later.

One of the reasons why it still seems to me important is that the
cultural élitism of which I accuse it in this essay remains with us, I
think. It has usually a less abrasive manner now, has learned a few
placative tricks and mock concessions but still lives, I believe, in a
good health that connotes, comparatively, the poorer cultural health
of many of those whose can't share in it. Another reason why I
believe in the continuing importance of the book is that I have never
found a more erudite or, much more important, a more intelligent
defence of that élitism.

I am aware of T. S. Eliot's criticism subsequent to *The Sacred
Wood*. I have decided to deal exclusively with *The Sacred Wood* for
two reasons. The first is that no criticism he wrote after *The Sacred
Wood* seems to me to overthrow the basic principles he was
outlining in this book. I detect in much of the later criticism a
mellowing of tone but no significant change of mind. He may
modify his voice a little but its pronouncements come ex the same
cathedra. Therefore, it seems fair to confront him in the precincts of
The Sacred Wood.

The second reason is a matter of personal history. When I arrived
at university as a first generation university student, I became
progressively dismayed at how much 'literature' seemed neither for
nor about most of the people I knew outside. As I suggested later, it
was like being asked to study a body of evidence in which ninety-odd
per cent of the witnesses were never called. The book that

crystallised my misgivings for me most fully was *The Sacred Wood*. This essay is partly an attempt to acknowledge that debt, since I think we are indebted to those who most clearly define what we can't agree with, because they oblige us to try to define our own positions.

The relevance of this to the poetry is that it might clarify what the poetry is not trying to do.

★

The very name — *The Sacred Wood* — is like a warning, implying a place where the uninitiated had better not venture. And so it proves. Here be mysteries, age-old rites the form and purpose of which are truly understood by a very few. One of them is our guide. But he is no chatty tour-operator who wants to show himself anxious to answer all our questions. He will simply tell us what he knows, realising before he speaks that most of us will not be able to grasp what he says. Given the nature of the place he believes himself to be and the attitude he has towards it, he would behave like that.

I first came across *The Sacred Wood* as an undergraduate. My mind went barefoot in awe and probably should have done. I was recently a schoolboy who had 'read a lot'. When the king of the paddling-pool sees his first ocean, awe is appropriate. Since then I have 'read a lot more' but I return to *The Sacred Wood* with that original awe not so much diminished as peopled by other considerations which are no longer content merely to gaze in wonder at the feeling but want to explore it and perhaps colonise it with questions.

★

Coming back to the book with my somewhat increased competence, I'm struck by two things: how often, where my judgment is adequate to the task, I agree with his observations on specific writers; a nagging worry about agreeing with him on anything. Mr Eliot has that effect on me.

I find his comments on Swinburne and Blake generally agreeable and illuminating. I have a clearer sense of Ben Jonson because of him. His remarks on *Hamlet* are interesting, even if they do seem a hardly adequate account of what is happening in the play, like a still photograph of an earthquake. His brief study of Marlowe's blank verse is arresting, if not wholly convincing. His seems a just assassination of Professor Murray. So where does the unease come from?

Part of it, of course, may relate to the unavoidable realisation that as a critic T. S. Eliot was a man of breathtaking pomposity, frequently giving the impression that he probably left not a note for the milkman but an illuminated manuscript.

'In a world which is chiefly occupied with the task of keeping up to date with itself, it is a satisfaction to know that there is at least one man who has not only read but enjoyed, and not only enjoyed but read, such authors as Petronius and Herondas. That is Mr Charles Whibley, and there are two statements to make about him: that he is not a critic, and that he is something which is almost as rare, if not quite as precious. He has apparently read and enjoyed a great deal of English literature, and the part of it that he has enjoyed most is the literature of the great ages, the sixteenth and seventeenth centuries. We may opine that Mr Whibley has not uttered a single important original judgment upon any of this literature. On the other hand, how many have done so?'

Still, Eliot himself was aware of this. In the preface to the 1928 edition, he says: 'especially I detect frequently a stiffness and an assumption of pontifical solemnity which may be tiresome to many readers. But these, like the other faults of the book, are too well diffused throughout to be amended. I should have to write another book.'

And, although apology isn't reparation, it would be churlish — in the light of his quality as a critic — to make too much of this. This can't be a serious objection, although it is perhaps a symptom of one.

The unease, though, persists. It surfaces from time to time in the way he quotes lines and knows you must see at once the point he is making about them and must agree. Sometimes I don't feel quite so sure.

'There is no conclusive evidence that he realised all the difference, the gulf of difference between lines like:

> En l'an trentiesme de mon eage
> Que toutes mes hontes j'ay beues;

and even the very best of Ronsard or Bellay, such as:

> Le temps s'en va, le temps s'en va, madame;
> Las! le temps, non, mais nous nous en allons
> Est tost serons estendus sous la lame.'

That, of course, is part of the Eliot critical method. That gulf is obvious to him. If it isn't to you, you're wrong and that's your problem. He intimidates with learning. He is, in his quiet pernickety way, an intellectual bully, less obstreperous with it than Pound but no less dismissive of possible opinions other than his own.

That assumptiveness extends to more general statements:

'Qua work of art, the work of art cannot be interpreted; there is nothing to interpret. . . .'

'The emotion of art is impersonal.'

'He has not the austerity of passion which can detect unerringly the transition from work of eternal intensity to work that is merely beautiful, and from work that is beautiful to work that is merely charming.'

I leave the first two to yourself. The third purports to be about Mr Whibley again, who has been unfortunate enough to incur Mr Eliot's praise. You may have noticed that it isn't about Mr Whibley at all. It is, by implication, about Mr Eliot. For how could Eliot see this lack in Mr Whibley, how could he even know such an amazing

quality resided in anyone if he didn't possess it himself?
And what is it, this amazing quality? It is an 'austerity of passion'.
It can 'detect unerringly'. It recognises 'work of eternal intensity'. It
is the process of patient erudition inexplicably transubstantiated
into a godlike capacity for judgment.

At the end of *Tradition and the Individual Talent*, Eliot says:
'This essay proposes to halt at the frontier of metaphysics or
mysticism, and confine itself to such practical conclusions as can be
applied by the responsible person interested in poetry.'

Eliot may speak in a quiet, meticulous voice but the statements it
makes patiently add up to an unexaminable belief in the basic
infallibility of his own judgment. He has erudition but the
conclusions it has brought him to are not seriously for questioning.
They have to be taken on trust, and that's the way he likes it. If it
weren't, he might not only pass judgment but pause to clarify it.

'But this is the case when such a man plants himself firmly in his
awareness of caste, when he says "The gentry must not abdicate". In
politics this may be an admirable formula. It will not do in literature.
The Arts insist that a man shall dispose of all that he has, even of his
family tree, and follow art alone. ... But there is only one man better
and more uncommon than the patrician, and that is the Individual.'

Eliot suggests somewhere that those things we read casually (like
advertising), when we are less on our guard, may get through to us
most effectively. Perhaps a corollary of that might be that those
things we write when we are least on our guard, when the subject
about which we are writing is someone to whom, say, we feel
superior, may reveal us most significantly.

The above quotation is from a section of *Imperfect Critics* called
'A Romantic Aristocrat'. The subject is George Wyndham. Mr
Wyndham is someone to whom Mr Eliot is offering, as he does to
Charles Whibley, what you might call a small pension of reputation,

nothing too substantial, just enough to let him eke out his immortality in a kind of genteel poverty of esteem.

These seem to me a very revealing few pages. It is from them that the 'gulf of difference' already quoted comes. It is also in this small essay that Eliot says:

'We cannot grapple with even the simplest and most conversational lines in Tudor and early Stuart drama without having diagnosed the rhetoric in the sixteenth- and seventeenth-century mind.'

Notice that he doesn't say that a knowledge of such rhetoric will enlarge our understanding or appreciation of those lines. He says that we cannot so much as 'grapple' (which is a pretty basic activity) with 'even the simplest' without 'having diagnosed' — a very weighty matter, indeed. Only scholars need apply. And then who's to say they'll get it right? Aware that he does sometimes tend to be exclusive, he makes a concession to non-scholars in *Tradition and the Individual Talent*: 'Shakespeare acquired more essential history from Plutarch than most men could from the whole of the British Museum.' Apart from the dubiousness of this statement, it can hardly be said to widen the field a lot. It still leaves most of us troglodytes hanging about outside, presumably reading the papers.

But it is in that part about the non-abdication of the gentry that what is going on here becomes clearest, as far as I'm concerned. And for me the key sentence is: 'The Arts insist that a man shall dispose of all that he has, even of his family tree, and follow art alone.'

To modify one of Mr Eliot's own statements: we have heard of this abandoning all for art before. And we didn't believe it then. For what does it *mean*? Does it mean materially? If so, I'm not aware of many great artists who did, outside of novelettes. Does it mean in some more spiritual way? If so, how can you tell what they abandoned?

But even if the truth of the statement were conceded, what would still dismay me about it is the tone of implied heroism. Borges says,

'Who can pretend to be merely an impostor?' By the same token, who can pretend to such purely high-minded motivation? What about the possibility that someone who chooses such noble dedication is so anaemic he'd rather do this than hassle with living as well? It seems to me mainly just another way of bolting the door on the plebs.

I don't think that Individual with a capital 'I' is just any individual. It may be an unworthy suspicion of mine that he is a patrician of letters, someone like T. S. Eliot or Ezra Pound or James Joyce. But, assuredly, there aren't too many of him to the epoch.

He represents the malignant premise I think underpins Eliot's criticism, a kind of literary capitalism: your heritage belongs to me because you wouldn't know what to do with it and I'm the man with the erudition in the bank.

This attitude seems to me something which permeates *The Sacred Wood*. I suspect that it comes from a quite impossible high-mindedness, a kind of lay sanctimony of the self-elect, further expressed, for example, in:

'The two directions of sensibility are complementary; and as sensibility is rare, unpopular, and desirable, it is to be expected that the critic and the creative artist should frequently be the same person' (*The Perfect Critic*).

The belief in this mutually sustaining clique which the artist makes of himself (with the possible inclusion of such others as prove 'rare' enough) may not have been invented by Eliot but The Sacred Wood is assuredly one of the books of its apocryphal bible. It is a belief which was one of the basic tenets of what has been called modernism:

> I join these words for four people,
> Some others may overhear them,
> O world, I am sorry for you,
> You do not know these four people.
>
> (Ezra Pound, *Causa*)

Anyone who, being told this, can give such an attitude mind-room has abdicated his brains.

★

The Sacred Wood is the work of Eliot as critic, not as poet. The separation of the two functions is one insisted on by Eliot himself: 'This gives us an intimation why the artist is — each within his own limitations — oftenest to be depended upon as a critic; his criticism will be criticism, and not the satisfaction of a suppressed wish — which, in most other persons, is apt to interfere fatally.' (*The Perfect Critic*)

This is a statement which has a pleasing neatness and is quite unverifiable. Still, that is the nature of comments on the arts, where educated assurance of assertion must stand in for the absent possibility of proof. In relation to this statement, I would make my own assertion: such separation as he implies would have to be questioned insofar as he uses the criticism as a mechanism for the release of the poetry, a self-conscious means of clearing the way for the poetry to happen as he thinks it should.

He may not be writing surrogate poetry when he criticises but he will presumably be justifying by implication his own poetry when he does so. Unless the poet-critic is inhumanly self-disciplined or has discovered the means of spontaneous cloning, his poetry and his criticism will be interdependent in this very significant way.

The implied disinterestedness, the claimed purity of response have to be questioned. In *Tradition and the Individual Talent* Eliot refers to 'my programme for the metier of poetry'. I find it questionable that a practising poet who has evolved such a programme should claim, when he looks at other poetry, to be seeing more purely what is there than someone who is solely a critic. I should suspect that he is more liable not to see what isn't there (which he suggests the critic may), but to fail to see what is there if it doesn't conform to the terms of his programme.

The question appears to be more complicated than Mr Eliot perhaps allows. For all those academic critics who engage in acts of conspiratorial pedantry with the writer of their choice, evincing galaxies of significance from atoms of meaning, there are all those poet-critics who see only what they need to see to prop up their own creative prejudices, reacting the way Auden confesses to when looking at another writer: 'My God! My Great-Grandfather! My Uncle! My Enemy! My Brother! My Imbecile Brother!'

The unaligned layman might do well to be suspicious of both, keeping with him as a kind of compass in the weedy wilderness of literary opinion the certain knowledge that art is usually more arbitrary than either its practitioners or its commentators admit.

There have, of course, been critical reappraisals since Eliot's criticism. But I believe the assumptively dominant minds in these matters are still those conditioned by the aesthetics of élitism which Eliot championed.

There are obvious reasons why this should be so. The people who have a voice in establishing the fashionable criteria, who pronounce publicly on what is good and what is bad, are themselves an élite. They are poets and critics and university men. It is, therefore, not surprising that their preferences should tend towards the intellectually arcane and the experientially effete. Such poetry mirrors many of their own lives. Then again they are likely to be a very conservative group, having invested heavily in career-shares of long established stock. Fluctuating markets worry them.

What *Dire Straits* call 'a whiff of the street' is seldom their favourite smell. The questionable image of T. S. Eliot, prim and clerical, pontificating on the wildness of Villon, one of life's dishevelled vagrants, like a chemist analysing a cupful of cataract and purporting to give you the essence of the phenomenon, is one paradigm of academia. Further, there is no surer way to put in

suspension the commonsense of academics (a commodity sometimes in short supply among them because so many of them in a
sense make a career of disproportion, a living from obsession) than
to intimidate them by having more learning than they have. What
you do with the learning will be of less importance than the fact
that you have it. What I think T. S. Eliot has done with his in
The Sacred Wood is to use it quite deliberately as a weapon
against those who have less. I see him as a monopolist of literary
heritage.

Such élitism might be said to be inevitable. Eliot himself has said,
'for there is no method except to be very intelligent'. That seems fair
enough but it does leave unanswered the not unimportant question
of what constitutes intelligence. I can't answer it either. I can only
affirm my belief in two of its crucial pivots: the continuing capacity
for growth that is oiled by self-doubt and some awareness of the
dimensions of the ignorance your knowledge inhabits.

Anyone who, in matters so open, can trust his own judgment to
the extent that Eliot does isn't to be trusted himself. And that
'ignorance' doesn't just apply to books; it applies to the nature of
experience as well, which is, after all, the proper subject of poetry —
not 'truth' but a true sense of ourselves, the only kind of truth we can
seek to inhabit without hypocrisy.

'The end of the enjoyment of poetry,' Eliot says in *The Perfect
Critic*, 'is a pure contemplation from which all the accidents of
personal emotion are removed. ...' I wonder who could achieve such
a condition. I doubt that Eliot ever did. I don't know a single human
being I can imagine reaching such a state of mind. It seems to me
literary mysticism: I can imagine the attempt but not the achieve-
ment and I think we should always suspect the impossible ideal —
it's a way of blinding us to the possible, so that we lose our share of
it.

Imagine a bon viveur of massive influence, a prophet of the

palate, a gastronomic Billy Graham. He has, through years of tasting and trying and purification of his taste buds, concluded that veal is the finest food, the only meat for the truly discriminating. He disseminates his wisdom. The food-purveyors of many countries hearken to his words. Think how many people with a taste for steak would have to forego it. Think how many people with no taste for veal would be turned off altogether. And it wouldn't help the experience of cattle a lot either. To convince a lot of its practitioners and critics that poetry is an activity for the élite doesn't just falsify their own tastes, sending them in pursuit of a bloodless refinement, it kills the potentiality for a more varied taste in others. For there is nothing to feed it. To insist that sensibility is such a rare, rare thing is a demand for philistinism in others. You are, after all, giving them no option.

Something analogous to this has been done, I believe, by Eliot and others who have come to poetry with a similarly religious zeal, as if it were an escape from human nature and not an intensification of our sense of it. The tendency seems all the more regrettable to me because it has coincided with the growth of other media which have been making it progressively harder for poetry to get much of a hearing anyway. Perhaps the inroads made by these other media into its sacred domain constitute one of the reasons why poetry has turned in on itself, become to some extent a cabal of poets talking to themselves. Maybe it's the pedants' revenge on all those parvenu art-forms. If so, it's about as logical as going on the attack by committing suicide.

A time when cinema and television and popular music were making great progress as majority media seems to me a time when poetry might have been trying to see what relevant voice it could still have in a more complicated dialogue. Perhaps T. S. Eliot, publishing in 1920, can be forgiven his ignoring of other media and his one sniffy reference to the existence of an art-form other than literary in *The Possibility of a Poetic Drama*: 'a mute theatre is a possibility (I do not mean the cinema).' But it remains ironic that while he was intoning his highly personal interpretation of the scriptures ('For mine is the kingdom', 'Blessed are the few') in his sacred wood, the trees were being chopped down round about him.

★

Yet *The Sacred Wood* remains a very valuable book. For one thing, to be in the company of an intelligence as fine and as disciplined as T. S. Eliot's can only do us good, provided we keep our wits about us and don't blink once. To appreciate the concentration and seriousness with which Eliot looks at literature you only have to turn, say, to W. H. Auden's essays in *The Dyer's Hand*. Read, for example, the first two pages of his essay on Byron's *Don Juan* to see that his critical intelligence is essentially frivolous and the rest of it to see that it is assuredly intelligence. In comparison to Eliot, Auden is a dandy of ideas, concerned more with the cut of his thought than the substance it contains.

A second reason follows for me from this one. In *The Sacred Wood* Eliot formulates more forcefully and clearly than any other critic I know what might be called the capitalist aesthetic of literature. Its criteria work to exclude as many people as possible. Its general effect is to teach most of us that our lives can at best provide fodder, raw material for that marvellous art which will eventually feed the esoteric sensibilities of a very few. Eliot lets us have it admirably straight, with no misleading mock concessions, no politic rhetoric for the plebs. What the devil, he won't speak 'em fair. He's the Coriolanus of critics.

★

If, like me, you feel yourself ranked among the plebs who confront Coriolanus, if you identify with the vague and partially inarticulate many whom Eliot rather loftily dismisses, whom he declares in his patrician way to be inevitably excluded from the 'end' of poetry, you've got problems.

Anyone who, like me, wants to suggest an alternative approach to poetry, to postulate the exploration of what might be called a socialist aesthetic (which might simply mean a way of appreciating poetry that keeps its contribution to our understanding of ourselves accessible to many more people than at present) will have to proceed with discipline. Flabby liberal sentiments about the rights of readers will not do. If you want to breach that sanctum, vaguely egalitarian impulses aren't enough. Nor is happy proletarian philistinism. It's no good trying to throw bricks through the window. It doesn't have any windows. It's no good shouting obscenities. Nobody can hear you in there. It's no good storming it with screwtops. It's too well guarded. You have to learn the passwords.

And there's a danger in that. The key password to that sanctum is 'sensibility'. What is it? How can it be acquired? It isn't easy to define. It's something vague. It has to do with intelligence, certainly. What *can* be said about it is that only those who have it can recognise it and it is utterly individual. It is presumably acquired from the process of applying intelligence rigorously to the reading of literature, preferably all literature.

There's the danger. The process of acquiring such sensibility is a process of isolation, leaving you able to identify in literary terms only with the few who share it. The only way to gain access to the sanctum is to become one of its guardians. It is analogous to the classic dilemma of revolutionary politics: how do you penetrate the modes of established power without becoming a part of them? How can you make such ideas a part of your system and preserve immunity to their élitist effects?

It's a problem compounded by the intimidatory effect of established systems. Eliot's interpretation of the past is fait accompli. He may say 'the past should be altered by the present as much as the present is directed by the past' (*Tradition and the*

Individual Talent) but, given the fixity of that past as he conceives it and demands that it must be, any possible alteration seems about as dynamic as repositioning some of the parts of an ambiguous jigsaw. Anyone trying to penetrate to the core of such critical theory to test the possibility of an alternative aesthetic finds, in the nature of things, that he has to confront an elaborate structure of postulated certainties, ostensibly hallowed with time, with a hopefully fructifying doubt. It's a hard struggle, like pitting a dream against masonry. Imagine a sensitive Visigoth (if, of course, you can't imagine such a thing, the dream will be one you can't have in the first place) arriving alone in a perfectly intact Roman villa. Won't the various mysterious facilities be awesome? Will it not be easier for him to take lessons from a Roman in their uses than to try and find out for himself and perhaps discover new inventive purposes? And won't the comfort they afford him be likely to make a Roman of him? And might his conclusion not be that only such Visigoths as become Romans are full participants in his culture? The significance of the Visigoths will become that they are not Romans.

For sophisticated assurance, no matter how dishonestly arrived at, has an apparent dignity of presence that honest doubt will seldom achieve. In such a presence honest doubt is all too likely to feel itself naked among the well dressed and put on borrowed precepts to cover its reality, simply because the other is so commandingly *there*. Too reverential an awareness of the past, of how it has been done, will habituate the potentially new voice at best into imitation, at worst into silence. I've known many university students who came to university with the determination to write and lost it there because the became intimidated by their awareness of what had already been written. They lost their belief in the primacy of experience.

It seems to me that the primacy of experience (the need for literature to judge itself not merely on its own closed terms of beauty

and rhythm and form but most importantly in terms of how far it
expresses and clarifies the realities of our lives as we have to live
them) is in much need of acknowledgement. One thing the advance
of a medium like television has done is to make all of us far more
conscious of the bewildering varieties, frequently hardly tolerable, of
human experience. Such an awareness is no longer just a concept in
the mind of an experienced and sensitive person. We are
bombarded with it daily. In the light of that, poetry as a privately
cultivated ornamental garden of the spirit seems to me
unacceptable. I think the literary idealism of the past is past.

But the hold it has on our consciousness and on the view we have
of literature is still present. The critical method of T. S. Eliot and
others forms a very effective security system against the invasion of
their privacy by others, leaving them in peace to enjoy the 'end' of
poetry. I think poetry has potentially other ends than the one to
which they put it. I think poetry is required for other uses by a great
many more people. I think, in order to free it effectively so that we
can begin to test its efficacy to meet those uses, we have to try and
dismantle that security system.

★

'On the other hand, poetry as certainly has something to do with
morals, and with religion, and even with politics perhaps, though
we cannot say what.' (Preface to the 1928 edition of *The Sacred
Wood*.) Like the make-up of an actor, the statement isn't meant to
be obtrusive. It is made and forgotten about and it should allow us
more effectively to accept the terms of the rest of the book.
Thereafter, poetry will be presented as 'poetry and not another
thing'. (Preface to the 1928 edition.)

The desire to maintain this clinical isolation of the phenomenon
of poetry is understandable, especially in someone who refers to 'the
pernicious effect of emotion' (*The Perfect Critic*) and to the fact
that social emancipation crawled abroad' (*Euripides and Professor*

Murray). Poetry may be 'excellent words in excellent arrangement and excellent metre' (Preface to the 1928 edition). The difficulty is that that excellence isn't autonomously decided by the words and the arrangement and the metre in independent conclave. Their relationship to our experience is somewhat relevant. Poetry is an adjunct of life or it is nothing. It only lives through an immensely complicated relationship with our experience. That relationship has many aspects more dynamic than 'pure contemplation'. To isolate poetry in this way, to seek rigorously to refine away its natural impurities to achieve this 'end' of 'pure contemplation' is like auditioning for the role of the mad scientist in an old Hollywood movie ('I haf discovered ze secret of poetry. All ze stanzas vill belong to me'). Once you build a laboratory round poetry, the only kind of investigation left to carry out is an autopsy.

The error lies in that phrase 'though we cannot say what', which is the sound of the laboratory door closing. It is true that we cannot say what, and it is the fact that we cannot say what which calls in question so much of what Eliot and others think they *can* say. It is precisely what we cannot say, what is unknown that for a serious application of intelligence is not dismissible. It is precisely that capacity of the known to qualify its stance in relation to the unknown that constitutes the continuance of intelligence.

I think Eliot's sense of tradition, judged against that criterion, is morbid. In spite of his remark that 'the past should be altered by the present', I cannot see the signs that he believed in this in any significant way. His sense of the past is of something to be submitted to with a terrible rigour in order 'to ponder collaboration to the utmost line . . . to distil the last drop of it [this pleasure], to press and press the essence of each author . . .' (*Philip Massinger*). Why? To be a dutiful servant to other people's pasts? What about the present and the future? Is our chief function as readers to revivify that past through our understanding and appreciation of it? Pharoah lives: let us labour to make pyramids of appreciation to house the great dead spirits of the past. Aren't we as well to loot them, each of us as best we can?

Even looters, of course, should be discriminating. In trying to achieve that discrimination, we will have recourse to some of the techniques Eliot makes use of. But need we apply them in the same ways or to the same ends? Erudition itself, the basis from which he starts, has a value that shifts in relation to the intelligence and experience that inform it. Cultivated for its own sake, it becomes merely a morbid hobby which can lead to a kind of inflation of the intellect. The more self-consciously esoteric it becomes, the more carefully the mind should ingest it, like a potentially unhealthy diet, because it can encourage you to form unearned opinions free from the vigorous opposition of other minds, giving rise to an inert complacency. The metabolism that transforms it into relevant energy is the intelligence, and that energy will seek dialogue.

Intelligence is the most crucial element in Eliot's critical method. It is, indeed, the method itself: 'for there is no method except to be very intelligent'. This intelligence is, of course, separate from the erudition. Knowledge is never intelligence; it is what intelligence reacts to; the way in which intelligence reacts is how it shows itself. A man with much less knowledge than another may not only be more intelligent but may often demonstrate the fact. I would suggest that for intelligence knowledge is most significantly a means of more precisely getting a fix on what it doesn't know, so that it locates the way in which it may grow; that intelligence is most properly gauged by the (intellectual) justice and honesty and skill with which a mind can inhabit its own inevitable ignorance.

Eliot, of course, is referring to intelligence as it applies to language. The first indication of morbidity I find in his sense of this intelligence and how it applies itself is the assumption he seems to make that it must of necessity remove itself from any very wide or significantly public dialogue. The energy seems, first of all, turned inward and at best shared only with a few like minds. That seems to me a singularly undynamic application of intelligence based on a quite unwarranted assumption. Where does the idea come from that the highest expression of critical intelligence lies in understanding or appreciating what very few can understand or appreciate? What is literature — some kind of eleven-plus of the spirit?

Intelligence as it relates to language inhabits an area with a characteristic that distinguishes it from, say, the sciences. It operates in a public domain, is a commodity of which almost everyone has some knowledge, is a consciously deployed factor in all our lives. Therefore, I'd suggest that linguistic intelligence is properly measured not just by its capacity to articulate but by its capacity to communicate. Writers may begin by talking to themselves but that self-articulation contains an implicit dialogue. A relevant criterion must be the extent of that dialogue, the extent to which the writer can make his words comprehensible and relevant to and concerned with as many people as possible while sacrificing as little as possible of the complexity of what he is trying to articulate.

The remit any writer takes on isn't merely to 'have been there', as Americans say, to have undergone with understanding the extremes of internal experience (whether you see that in terms of Hemingway-Mailer machismo or the more spiritual contemplation of someone like Eliot). It is also to have come back. Like the black box in an aeroplane crash, the writer's function is not just to discover the nature of experience but to bring back an expression of what it is like that is relevant to the experience of as many others as possible.

The width of that relevance seems to me crucially important. The more people to whose appreciation you can honestly submit your findings, possibly the more validly they are tested, because just as experience is shared by all of us, some significant appreciation of the expression of it is potentially so. Such appreciation can't be total, of course. It has limitations. But it should at least be an important principle of writing that the writer should not wilfully or self-indulgently preclude the wider possibilities of that appreciation. The complacency with which Eliot accepts the inaccessibility of the best poetry seems to me a narrowing of the craft's potential. Such an attitude has rubber-stamped a fair amount of charlatanism in modern poetry, arcane utterances that merit Roy Campbell's comment *On Some South African Novelists:*

> 'You praise the firm restraint with which they write.
> I'm with you there, of course.
> They use the snaffle and the curb all right.
> But where's the bloody horse?'

The attempt to achieve such appreciation and relevance must remain, of course, something which involves the reader in effort as well as the writer. There can never be a licence for the reader — no matter how intelligent — to say, 'I don't immediately appreciate this, therefore it isn't any good.' And in trying to find a just compromise between the necessarily difficult and the wilfully inaccessible, the controlling vote must be with the writer. The inevitable arbitrariness of art, the way in which it is for so many writers — and perhaps for all writers of originality — the pursuit of a personal daimon, must not be legislated against. But anyone who tries to write will equally inevitably find himself or herself trying to learn control of that impulse to write. One of the key components of that machinery of control will be the maintained determination to make his or her writing as accessible as he or she honestly can, or the writer will have sacrificed integrity. 'Great problems are in the street,' Nietzsche says. I think writers should try as far as possible to put the words that seek to deal with them in the same place.

Of course, the question of accessibility has to remain an open one for every writer as he works. But for the critic it does admit of judgment, albeit difficult judgment. Whatever creativity is, it has much to do with achieved clarity.

It is difficult to arrive at any guiding principle for assessing how just, how earned the difficulty of a poem or a piece of prose may be.

But I would think that fairness to the reader has to be a relevant criterion. No matter what private beliefs in the sanctity of art or divine inspiration or the priestliness of his task a writer may draw his initial energy from, he had better remember what he is trying to do when he applies it. He is trying to communicate with others. To do that effectively, he will be concerned not only to delcare where he is but to direct that declaration towards where they are.

Where they are most significantly, if he reaches them at all, is reading his work. This means that any serious difficulty he presents them with should be resolvable within the terms of the work itself as it relates to their intelligence and experience. This doesn't mean that no work should make allusions to any other work. Almost all poetry does so, however indirectly. What will matter is that such allusions shouldn't be necessary to give the new work coherence, to justify its existence. Otherwise, it has no significant existence. The allusions may be a kind of incidental decoration or they may, more importantly, be so subsumed in the whole that they achieve a new and independent life in it.

That respect paid to the active and present intelligence of the reader — as opposed to the hypocritical 'respect' of assuming that he or she must have read what you have read or must at least want to — is one guide to the difference between necessary difficulty and wilful obfuscation. It is a sign of dynamic intelligence to work for mutually meaningful confrontation with all other intelligences, not wilfully to choose forms of expression which preclude such confrontation. The latter is often no more than a ploy to establish intellectual status, to elicit from others a habit of intellectual respect your use of your intelligence doesn't justify.

Instead of taking on the burden of the communal experience more determinedly, instead of addressing itself to the problem of finding renewed relevance, of finding how to speak to, about and for the lives around it, poetry has often pursued a sterile aestheticism. For many people the most important criterion in measuring the development of a poet has become how fully he has explored his own technical virtuosity. How far he may have spoken relevantly to the times, how far he has contributed to the community's understanding of itself outwith the hothouse culture of the universities or the oxygen-tent conditions of a poetry-reading will be of less significance.

★

'He exercises neither of the tools of the critic: comparison and analysis' (*Imperfect Critics*). As far as I have been able to determine from my reading of *The Sacred Wood*, what Eliot means by the tools of the critic is 'comparison with his own other work and with the work of other writers' and 'analysis of linguistic effects'. We are back to poetry as 'poetry and not another thing'. But it is several other things: 'poetry as certainly has something to do with morals, and with religion, and even with politics perhaps, though we cannot say what'. That being the case, how can 'comparison and analysis' be justifiably or even meaningfully limited in these ways?

It may, of course, create problems we cannot satisfactorily solve immediately to push the critical intelligence beyond these invented limits, but, according to Eliot's own principles, that should surely not deter us: 'And the free intelligence is that which is wholly devoted to inquiry'. That's fine. It presumably means that such inquiry will not confine itself to questions so carefully limited as to be merely molten answers. Yet the questions Eliot's critical intelligence sets itself are in a very real sense 'rhetorical'. They are about words in self-containment, considered as a self-governing body. As such, they don't make poetry more alive for us, they embalm it. To do more than this, 'comparison and analysis' would have to be made to extend their application, no matter what difficulty or trepidation that involves for the applicant. 'Comparison' would centrally involve 'comparison with apprehended experience' and 'analysis' would most importantly include 'analysis of the honesty of the work's relationship to experience.

★

Eliot's reverential contemplation of the past is, I have suggested, morbid. It is so determined to achieve what looks like a literary equivalent of transcendental meditation that it mortifies the present, rendering its poetic potential anorexic. Hence, perhaps, *The Waste Land*, that impressive echo-chamber poem, where, to achieve dramatic stature, his own times have to be buskined in old quotations, masqued in allusions. I don't think Eliot is significantly describing the post-war world so much as he's describing his own culture shock. I see the deeper, accidental meaning of *The Waste Land* as being not that things were so different but that the ability to pretend that they were is on the way out. The stature of the past and of the men of the past was always a myth. By the time Eliot wrote *The Waste Land* it was a disintegrating myth. His poem is one of poetic idealism's last stands, and for me not a particularly heroic one. Instead of trying to look steadily through the hole history has blown in the pretensions poetry had for so long allowed itself, he papered it over with nice quotations, and jacked up those pretensions ever higher.

What I think Eliot is reacting against in *The Waste Land* and in his criticism is what much modern poetry has reacted against. They may call it 'decline in standards' or 'loss of values' or just plain 'philistinism'. Not a few modern artists and appreciators of the arts see themselves as standing out against the vulgar tastelessness of so much modern life. Poets, I suspect, are particularly prone to this romantic misconception. (Consider the first words quoted in this essay from *The Sacred Wood*.)

Like *The Waste Land*, what they are holding out against is, I believe, the most significant literary event of this century. This event isn't a series of novels or the career of a great writer or a school of poets or a critical theory. It's only 'literary' in the sense that if affects drastically and probably irrevocably the status of literature in our culture. The event is simply that our society has become culturally open.

The relative importance of the various factors contributing to this condition is debatable; even what these factors may be could be debated: international upheaval; social emancipation 'crawling' abroad; a decline in the intellectual status of religion; perhaps even the way in which Marxism has tried to arrange a shotgun wedding between Western society and the idealistic philosophy it had maintained for so long as its mistress — that has certainly been one traumatic experience. What I would have thought isn't seriously debateable is that poetry, obliged to live in the midst of such a cultural hubbub, such a jostling and unresolved confusion of cultural values, renders any contribution it might make largely invalid by entrenching itself in purely aesthetic criteria, by defining itself as 'a superior amusement' ('Preface to the 1928 Edition').

Surrounded by change, faced with the emergence of new modes of communication, bewildered by the now much more openly acknowledged varieties of life as it is lived, confronted with the collapse of its own spurious idealism, finding the closed assumptions of its past no longer tenable — what should poetry do? Eliot's answer is chillingly simple. It should close those assumptions further. Since the public is such an unappreciative rabble, poetry should not concern itself with them. Let it develop the sensibilities of the few.

'Individual sensibility' is, he would say, what poetry is for. And what is individual sensibility for? It is for itself, its own 'pure contemplation'. Perhaps it could hardly be for much else, since it is so rare. It is, of course, the appreciative counterpart to that creative man 'The Arts' insisted should 'dispose of all that he has, even of his family tree, and follow art alone'. (You will remember that 'the two directions of sensibility are complementary' and that sensibility is 'rare, unpopular, and desirable'.) It all makes for a rather romantic spiritual scenario: rare and lonely artist meets rare and lonely critic and from their union come rare and lonely 'pure contemplations'. And that sterile marriage is the hallowed 'end' of poetry? I'd rather not be a guest at that particular wedding.

But is sensibility in either of its complementary forms necessarily such a limited phenomenon? I think a lot of significant art *does* have its origins in the kind of loneliness Eliot implies. I think a lot of serious writers do suffer in something like the way that Eliot suggests. But I also think that 'The Arts insist' is a rather hazily romantic explanation to append to that loneliness and that suffering. A harder look might yield a less Eleusinian response.

First of all, I dont think that isolation of the artist is something that he will work at, as if it were part of his craft. Or if it is so cultivated, he will be a poser. The lonely suffering the artist undergoes is inevitable, if it is there at all. It's the thing about himself he can't avoid. If it is 'insisted' upon, it can't be real. It's as likely to happen to him if he's holed up in the Hilton on an expense account as anywhere else. It's presumably what found Descartes in Amsterdam, what pursued Kafka from Prague to Berlin.

I'm not saying it's some birthmark of the Muses. I should think it's an acquired characteristic. I just don't think that it is ever successfully acquired deliberately. And although its acquisition isn't achievable under laboratory conditions, I don't think where it comes from need be any great mystery. It comes, I believe, from an individual's compulsive need to codify his own experience for himself without intermediaries, to shape it for himself into a comprehensible para-experience, to recreate reality into a unity his actual experience didn't achieve. The artist suffers because he is trying to effect a painful rebirth. He is lonely because his compulsion precludes him from merely accepting who he is and sharing it with others. That is a very practical loneliness.

And why should the compelled nature of his isolation not make him seek as wide a communication as possible through his art? Perhaps only a dilettante of that isolation would be happy to extend it into his art by wilfully and complacently excluding people from it. His isolation will be how he earns his gift; his ability to share it will be how he expresses it.

And if the quality of sensibility in the artist needn't be judged by how patricianly dismissive he is of the importance of wide appreciation, why should the quality of sensibility in the critic be judged by how incommunicable it is to most other people? Critical sensibility is also acquired in loneliness, it is true, because it develops in a vigorous eliciting of your own responses, in a refusal to pretend to feel or think merely what you ought to feel or think, in a censoring in yourself of mimicry or imitation, in a discovery of honesty to self. But the very quality of that honesty will depend on how far you succeed in bringing to that confrontation between you and the thing read the sense of others who are not present, even of those who are incapable of being present (like the illiterate), by how far you can make the privacy of your head as public as possible.

Sensibility can be a growing capacity to identify emotionally and intellectually with more and more people. If it is so far what Eliot says it is, it might be a good idea to find out how to change it.

It is very difficult to achieve any just sense of what poetry is. I can think of a couple of reasons for this. The first is that its dominant characteristic is its variousness. Like a kaleidoscope, it fulfils itself by not staying the same. You may describe the structure and the principles of a kaleidoscope but the essence of it is that you don't know what it will do, what will be there when you look into it. The second is that, like so many of the arts, poetry gives rise to some terrible nonsense, boastful ravings of no ascertainable substance. With the possible exception of sex, the arts are perhaps the area where most lies are most glibly told.

These two reasons are not unconnected. The very vagueness of the boundaries of poetry, the volatility of any attempt to define its 'function', the inevitable uncertainty of judgments passed as to comparative quality in it, all conspire to make it a potentially happy hunting-ground for ideas that aren't always reputable. Like a small independent state the laws of which are vague and the customs of which are not notoriously stern on contraband, it welcomes to its bosom some strange theories whose papers of identity look distinctly home-made. These we can find sojourning in the land of poetry and sometimes living high on fake currency.

Given that problem, it's perhaps understandable that an intelligence as fastidious as Eliot's should withdraw behind a structure of lofty principles, admitting only those whose credentials he regards as unquestionably authentic. He had, after all, the rhyming gossip of Georgian poetry to react against. (Perhaps one way to see *Prufrock* is as a marvellously ironic extension of that poetry, trivia in overdrive.) But more important than any under-standable motivation seems to me the effect Eliot has had on subsequent attitudes to poetry by making himself, through the formidable force of his intelligence, a kind of Pierpoint Morgan of the word.

The lingering effect has been, I believe, to intensify the splitting of poetry into the private and the public sector, as it were. There have been good 'popular' poets since the impact of Eliot and Pound ('popular' in relation to poetry being a word we should use tentatively, since it connotes a ghetto of popularity within a large indifference). But such guerrilla outbreaks don't seem to me to have very significantly repaired the division between 'serious' poetry and 'popular' poetry.

I think a kind of intellectual hangover remains, a fog of assumptions: that the very best poetry is probably beyond the appreciation of all but a very few people; that the ultimate quality of poetry is perhaps measurable by this very fact; that for poetry to be finally serious it has to be first of all solemn; that obscurity is perhaps a prerequisite of depth; that immediacy of impact might be rather vulgar. Such assumptions would be pernicious enough if their total effect were to confine a lot of creative energy to what I have called the 'private sector'. But their effect goes further, I think. They damage the potential development of a virile popular poetic tradition.

One way in which this damage is done relates to my suggestion earlier that to define sensibility as such a rare, rare thing is a demand for philistinism in others. The kind of impossibly high-minded aesthetic Eliot puts forward can have the effect — by cutting all but the most 'serious' poetry off without a cultural penny — of relieving popular poetry of its responsibilities to meet any significant aesthetic standards at all. A 'popular' movement like the 'Beat poets' seems to me a demonstration of this effect. You don't need to have the severity of vision of T. S. Eliot to see their poetry as generally pretty bad — not because they haven't studied the tradition of the medieval troubadours but simply because when they come to the page they use words vaguely and lack form. I don't think they're an isolated phenomenon. I think some of what passes for popular poetry today patronises its potential audience.

That, it seems to me, is not to combat those assumptions mentioned previously, but to condone them. It is to make a kinder-garten of the possibility of a popular poetry while the grown-ups get on with the real stuff. I think any attempt to move towards a healthy popular poetry would involve the reader in real effort. But, hopefully, the effort would bring rewards because the poetry wouldn't be an expression of lofty indifference towards most readers but an attempt to engage in a dialogue, even if an inter-mittently complicated dialogue, with the lives of people around it. It wouldn't seek to be merely a 'superior amusement'. It wouldn't accept the inevitability of Auden's statement: 'poetry makes nothing happen'. (*In Memory of W. B. Yeats*, a good poem which for me makes several things happen.)

For, surely, poetry does make something happen. The problem is that it isn't easy to define what poetry makes happen and impossible to legislate for how it makes it happen. For these things happen in the sensibility of the reader or listener. They are insights, illuminations, pleasures, sympathies, unexpected recognitions, understood griefs, new awarenesses, changed ways of seeing, confirmations of the half-felt, wonder at the familiar, renewed possibilities. There is more but this already seems to me quite a lot for poetry to make happen. It is exactly this capacity of poetry to intensify our awareness of being alive, to sharpen our sense of our shared humanity that makes its use as some status symbol of an élite so unacceptable.

To fulfil effectively the things it can do, I should have thought poetry has to try to make itself relevant to and accessible to the 'sensibility' of as many people as possible. It shouldn't fear the compromise of its principles. In giving itself a function alongside television or cinema or rock music, it would remain itself. For literature still contributes to the development of individual sensibility — and therefore to the potential development of communal sensibility — an element that no other medium of communication can supply. Literature remains a do-it-yourself phenomenon for the reader, demanding exercise of the imagination, acknowledgement of complexity, honest thought, education of the feelings. And poetry especially involves these.

I can't see anything sacred about poetry. But the structure's there with all its facilities and, as always, there's a cultural war on. It could perhaps be commandeered for more practical purposes. If it's no good as a temple, it might make a useful field dressing station.

★

I'm aware that such an essay as this is like Caesar running all the way to the Capitol, especially when what it precedes is in part an experiment in trying to appropriate for poetry some of the techniques of the novel and the cinema. But I believe in the attempt.

These Words:
Weddings and After

These Words: Weddings and After

I

Dearly beloved, we are gathered here—

Oh, what a voice he has! He *loves* that voice.
The monotony of eternity is there.
It offers resigned ears no other choice
But to surrender reason—

In the sight of God
And in the face of this congregation—

They're going down already. Their eyes glaze
The drug is working. Sense becomes a blur
In which all edges haze,
Meaning and nonsense shake hands and are friends
And many impossibilities can occur
And one's occurring now—
Eternal faith from perishable vow—

To join together this man and this woman—

The voice is its own purpose and goes on.

But sound's not meaning and we are
In contradiction's element,
Ever-moving in the word
That's motionless around ferment,
Goldfish swimming in a jar.

The duet of official love
Convention makes but people live
Is sung again. The backing choir
Of well-trained preconceptions swells
Its technical accompaniment.

The hallelujah moods intone
That two are now becoming one.

But those not numbed by repetition
Can catch perhaps an undersong
That improvises on the theme
Of dreams that go where dreamers can't,
An unplanned, sobbing, small descant
That casually breaks hearers' hearts.

It is the sound of being human
Of being man and being woman
And looking for a way to meet
That will forgive our difference.

No structured prison of response
Can ever quite confine that demon
Revenge on form that content takes.
It is the truest sound we make,

Experienced truth, to which all lies translate.

These Words: Weddings and After

Do you, stranger among strangers,
Take this stranger for your own
In strangeness and in strangerness?

Do you accept this weird convention
Where we immure your good intention
And don't care how it fares?

Do you, man, mouth these platitudes
Of idealised, unlikely good
And perhaps disprove them afterwards?

And do you, woman, say these words
Though they seem patently absurd,
Male prejudice in fancy dress?

No way we took leads quite to here.

We met, you see, in separate dreams
And promises from magazines
And gradually we found ourselves
Upon a stair we hadn't built
Of aspirations we're not sure were ours.

A band was playing, not our song.
The chorus came. We sang along.
Is this where we should be? Are these guests ours?

No way we took seemed leading quite to here—

In matrimony, an honourable estate—

(Without thinking too much, Mary wed Tim
And May married Sam though she didn't know him
And they begat Sarah who married the son
Of Mary and Tim at the point of a gun
And they begat John, a creep with a sneer
Who proposed to Melinda over a beer
And they had a daughter they christened Janine
Who without ever knowing where he had been
Married Michael, called Mick, a smoothie and slick,
Suave, all in all a most plausible prick
And got on with begatting. By this time, of course,
The begetting was wild as a runaway horse.
All logic was lost in those multiple beds
Where genes ran like chickens without any heads.
The begetters begat the begetters of others
And only made daughters so they could be mothers
And sons were the fathers of fathers of sons
Of fathers of fathers of some other ones
And nobody halted this runaway steed,
Put on riding-habits and followed the lead.
Let's call it a train—it suits the sense better
As well as the rhythm from the first begetter.
This train of events, well out of control,
Was to stop at the church of St Pete-in-the-Hole
And here would alight in splendour immense
A clutch of strange guests, as if it made sense:
The minister's voice, the organ, the rice—
A wedding,
A wedding,
A wedding—how ni-i-c-ce!)

Do you Elizabeth Claire—

I do remember how we were.

On the beach we were heightened somehow
So it seemed, stilted on dunes,
Etched on a template of sea.
Was it our love of palming the eyes
That makes the sun appear to have been so brazen?

The struck gong of heat, that maddened perspective
Where the hair of a leg had the texture of rope
And an eye swam its exploding iris into your own.

The talk was a caste, the laughter was all assignations.
I've forgotten the names now, only
Some fragments of frieze in a mythic sun:
The boy's oiled and arching body
Hallooing the haze, the dark girl
Frying in puppy fat, the ball
Hung in the air, the faces
Fixed in their sun grins, heraldic and strange.

And do you, Tom—

I see us still both cut off in that storm.

I don't think you remember it. The rain
Did nothing to allay the wind,
The trees were roaring.
The night was someone else's quarrel
We were caught in.
You loaned me your umbrella.

I was edging home along a bluff of wind,
The darkness flapped and banged.
At the first corner
Your umbrella flupping outside in.

I seemed knocking on the air, your house so wind-wrapped
And when you opened
Why were we such strangers?
Our intimacy washed off with your makeup.
Alone there in the still eye of that anger
A stranger gave a strange thing to a stranger.

That instant quarrel
About something that had happened days ago,
About everything about us,
Each beating against each other's sheer aloneness
Like a salmon trying to jump Niagara.
I was drenched in utter comprehension,
Knew my element impossibility.

On up the road, 'For Christ's sake,' I was saying,
'Jesus Christ.'
The wind seemed bending houses, juggling trees.

In the chip-shop the small, taut man was closing,
His mouth trying to unwind in a yawn.
'Had a guid nicht, son?' giving me cigarettes.
'No' bad,' I said.
Since then we've been our secret.

The earned dimension:
How often afterwards the endless falls—
Witless with thunder,
Slung on that wild parabola,
Needing to spawn.

48

Mirror on the dressing-table,
Gropings in the twilit park,
Wild underwear I never used,
Sage winks, that summer near the sea,
How did we get from you to here?

Mr and Mrs Grant MacWhirter
('Pompous oaf and manic flirter')

Request the pleasure (if it is
For we must ask some right ones here.
Does Uncle Davy *have* to come?
Not that old silly maiden saint
Who thinks none should because she can't?
And Mary's man? Oh, Jesus, no.
And Tom the talking vallium?
And Allison, that vicious bastard?
It's like inviting sheer disaster.
This list is sad and getting sadder.
They should elope. We'll buy the ladder.
Not Betty?) *of the company*

of

Mr and Mrs Strange Relations
(How the hell are they invited?
It's like the United bloody Nations.)

at the wedding of their daughter, Elizabeth Claire

49

(There, there, my love, there, there. There, there.

It's not how we imagined it.
It's not how we imagined it.
How is it that such dreams will come
To blown seeds in the winds of time
That grow a forest where we're lost?
Hope is the flower that finds a frost.

It's not how we imagined it.
Where does the laughter go that's laughed?
Where is the garden where she played?
Who opened the gate through which she passed?
Childhood's an empty swing at last
That creaks forever in the mind.

You love the dress that doesn't fit.
It's not how we imagined it.)

To–

(Strange are the names
Stuck on millions of doors
In lost housing-schemes.

Where do they come from, where do they go—
McLintock, Devanney, Milligan, Rice,
Adamson, Smith, Ellis, McLean,
Carruthers, Lucas, Stanley, Jones, Low?
They go on forever, that's where they go.
And they are all out there,
A vast otherness, a Visigoth army,
A difference from you,
Approaching, approaching. What will they do?

These Words: Weddings and After

At night you have heard them—
A shout in the street
Laugh fierce as a flame-thrower
Grenade of a curse
Machine-gunning fire of their running feet
Or silence. That silence! Their silence is worse.

And the duvet you've had for a year now looks strange.
Its pattern is sinister. Who designed that?
Who chose those pictures you have on the wall?
The clock's a fifth-column. That shadow's a rat.
How can a photograph suddenly change?
This isn't the address you should have been at.
When will the, when will the Visigoths call?

But you practise calmness, take a course of routine
So that time takes you only where you have been.
The mortgage is dwindling, the car's running well,
(When will the, when will the Visigoths call?)
The garden looks nice and the holiday snaps
Show everyone happy, there's business trips,
The firm's magazine last month had a glowing
(But when will the, when will the Visigoths call?)
Big double-spread on the great things you're doing,
Weather's improving, you're asked out to dine,
(But when will the, when will the—), everything's fine.

And in a still time
When nothing is wrong,
Your finances sing a harmonious song
And fear is asleep
And life seems a story
That you are inventing, a nice Jackanory
With an ending so happy a salesman would weep
And only makes promises that he might keep.
It happens, it happens, it happens to you.

The door to your fortress is opening now,
Not beaten down, no axe driven through.
It yields to the turn of a slily found key.
You look and are helpless—the Visigoth's there.
He'll eat at your table, he'll sit in your chair.
His eyes are dark tunnels you can't penetrate.
What will he do with the dreams you've amassed?
You do not know. Thought dwindles to one:
He is the future and you are the past.
As he clumsily gathers your future, you hear
Your daughter say, this is—)

Tom Docherty.

On a date that marks a trivial kind of death,
In a church, as suits an awesome act of faith.

RSVP
(Nice code-letters, foreignness
Dress naked doubts in politesse.)

Dreams that ravished lonely nights,
Experiments in double dark,
First menstruation, first love-bites,
What are these people thinking here?

Organ, organ, playing sombre,
Be our voluntary guide
Through the vaults of vague believing
To where we are seeing far
Past the fickleness we are.
Teach us that a room's a chamber
And that sin connotes a God.
On triter organs play, removing
The growth of pettiness that rots.
Fill us full of solemn thoughts.

I'm a spinster. I'm a doctor.
I'm a—who's that over there?
We consummate a long, slow stare.

These glances of longing, the mayflies of passion,
A quick tryst of strangers, a moment's affair,
Couplings of eyes that take place in mid-air,
Are textual gaps in the logic of lives.
Definitive versions will always elide them.
Lives like to pretend to semantic cohesion.
Such glances are wanton in their dissolution.
But if they had glosses they might mention

How truth incarnates in moments
That suck our blood to live
And give us in return the sharp grief
Of their joy and bruise of ecstasy,
The human mark— a love of what must die,
Indifference to immortality,
A large impossibility of heart
Where all that our humanity inherits
Is the sniper in the beauty of the trees,
The fatal ambushes of sunsets,
The shrouds of the bright waters, the shared glance.

God, this collar's killing me.
Stained glass window is a mess.
Thought this wedding was at three?
Piss on this. The music's hellish.
Voluntary? Yes, all right but
Do we need a liberty?

Organ, organ, write upon us
There's a God in whom we trust,
That daily, scribbled contradictions
Are agnostic palimpsest.

The tigers eat in smoke-filled rooms and rift philosophy.
The virgin has applied by post to keep the dragon's den.
The children play at ageing and the aged play at death.
The hallowed precepts murder men and bury God again.

The public ferret sniffs along the burrows of the mind.
Dipped in good faith, the words like sheep are flowing from
    the pen.
Their wallets stuffed with broken laws, the legislators laugh.
Lips of the poor bleed kisses and bury God again.

In libraries books count the dead and conjugate the storm.
One dignitary dresses in the skins of many men.
On midnight there is hammering a fear in uniform.
The corridors lead to corridors and bury God again.

The hands of malice have put on the gloves of rectitude.
The evil doctor's scalpel has been trademarked with the good.
The playgrounds of the flesh are lying empty in the rain.
The artist sells a painted scream. We bury God again.

What a hat there! I've a thirst
Could desiccate a brewery.
He's the best man? Who's the worst?
What price God? He's one-'n'-three.

Organ, organ, play our smallness
Into stature of the mind.
Break our windows' blurred striations
Till naked time rush in and we
May briefly sniff eternity.
Cure us of this mortal illness.

Bring our shipwrecked dreams to land
Where worth of self in wild plantations
Grows and never knows a blight.
Teach us to observe this rite.

Do you now promise one from two?

(No structured prison of response
Can ever quite confine that demon
Revenge on form that content takes.
It is the truest sound we make.)

I (think I think I think I) do.
I (don't think I can say I) do.

II

Here let the cynic sheathe his tongue.
Remove the clapper from the bell
Of public disbelief.
The thought that doesn't wish them well
In silence should be rung.
Believing in good is the good.

No raucous glibness here where two
Walk as the one somnambulist.

In slow procession, see, they come from ritual's amplitude
And wear their clothes like destiny. The aisle's a metaphor
Belongs to them alone. The watchers, crudely literal,
Stare and stare and try to be
Subsumed in this solemnity
But trivia buzz like flies around a throne.

Uncle Davy, former navy,
Thinks he feels one coming on—
Thunder-clapper there's no doubt—
Wants to bow but doesn't dare
In case he lets a ripper out.

He tries to beam through pursing lips
And thinks of anal Freudian slips.
Was his urge to blow a mock fanfare?

A broken marriage made him bitter.
For months he was distilling water
For his whisky from his eyes.

An architect, he draws plans where
The kind of life he'll never share
Can happen. But the true blueprint
He carries with him everywhere
No builder's skill will realise.

To build a house, forego the past absurd
That would ingest the future, leaves a turd
Of fabulous dimensions. Have the sense
To work in a makeshift present very tense.

Doorways you'll need to come, but more to go,
Ceilings that undulate from high to low
And walls that flap and rooms that shift their ground
Where friends are always strangers newly found.

The furniture is doubt, the kind of chair
That leaves you sitting neither here nor there,
A table that's unsteady and a bed
That never quite accommodates your head.

Make it for children. Adults have no place
Playing charades of permanence. With grace
Make it a part of you where children stay
Until they find themselves and walk away.

The watchers, crudely literal, stare at this deep, symbolic text
And find its meaning is elusive
And draw, since mind can't stop, effusive
Graffiti in the margins, vexed
That they are so peripheral
But pretend they understand the meaning that this time expects.

Auntie Margo is in prison
Looking out through chintzy bars.
It's a big one—cells are endless,
Detached house and restaurants,
Holidays in foreign places,
Deadly guests and fancy cars,
Hates the jailer whose last laugh
Meant there's no remission here.
Her sweet smile says, 'Welcome, dear.'

Welcome to a business booming
Since the paintings of Lascaux—
The art of magic decoration. Styles have changed.
Bison metamorphose to flying ducks
To pretty dogs to horses on the shore.
But the quarry has been constant. It has ranged
Through every city, several million books—
Content, the mythic mammoth that can give
Food for the soul, a painless way to live.

Life dies of its ideals. See all around
The graveyards of suburbia abound.
Lobotomised by faith, the walking dead
Rearrange the furniture and sit
Enduring rigor mortis of the head,
Amazed to find the monster. They are it,
A simple epitaph carved on their soul:
These caught a mammoth which then ate them whole.

The aisle's a path of metaphor where others here have gone
And some remember what they meant,
Find a pressed flower of sentiment
Crushed in the small print of a dusty tome.

When you went out today and I
Stood quiet in the quiet house,
Infinity was in a shell
And absence was rehearsing death.
I felt a grief I couldn't feel.
I knew the stopping of your breath.

Hold me, my love, while holding holds.
Around the edges of each place
The wolf of death is sniffing you.
While we can touch, we block that meeting—
The hole that my world will fall through,
Unplugged by every other greeting.

Oh, bathe our lives in ceremony's effulgence.
May the brideness of this woman
Like the magic of a shaman
Transmogrify our common places.
May her whiteness cleanse our failures
And the glow from her regalia
Rekindle hope in beaten faces.

Crazy Daisy, never lazy,
Purpose clear but reasons hazy,
Holds a world up and stays human,
Proves that Atlas was a woman,
Runs from age to age to age
In the same revolving cage,
Always moving, never stopping,
Bearing, caring, cooking, shopping
Because her life's a ticker-tape
Of where to be, of things to do,
Nurse the children, make the bed—
Will she ever meet herself?
And till it's over—here's a laugh—
She lives in her own epitaph:

For what she hasn't done she pays.
The window purples to a bruise.
She puts her body on like clothes.
She puts her worries on like shoes.

The news ignores her. She is glad.
She husbands bad to stave off worse.
She rubs a gentle itch of rooms.
She keeps horizons in a purse.

Alternatives are dust erased.
Familiar shops retail her life.
For what she hasn't done she pays.
For what she hasn't done she pays

And comes to weddings as her one indulgence.
Oh, bathe our lives in ceremony's effulgence.

Mystery is what they dare and awe like leaves is stirred
But in a daily cage of habit lives hope, the fabulous bird.
We must forgive it dowdiness and not judge it too hard
If when it learns to talk it parrots only what it's heard.

Molly Barker is a virgin,
Comes to weddings
Like a book by Mills and Boon,
Only needs to see one page
And at once begins to swoon.
Romance, romance, romance, romance—
Another dream, another chance.

She semaphores her dreams in wanton hats
And sublimates her passion in her cats.

Indoors they are the connoisseurs of sleep,
Contortionists of ease. Experiment
In modes of gentle pleasure seems career.
They make casual such wild postures, they could keep
Rest balanced on the points of carving knives—
Barely kinetic art. Poses appear
To melt into each other. They present
A show of peace, are sculptors of content.

Awake, a stylish waiting fills their lives.
Absorption in themselves explodes in tense
Harsh melodramas of no consequence.
They stalk a shoe-lace, kill stray balls of wool.
They seem to be rehearsing truth. The sense
Is of another self they just control.

Outside they find their métier: lust and death.
Their yowling satirises all they seem,
Makes houses wilderness, each bed a heath
And litters their brute truth on every dream:

Ferocities whose manners can be pretty,
Nice parables of domesticity.

Husband and wife there is. Out of uncertainty of two
Emerges mystic one. The aisle's a path of metaphor
Belongs to them alone. The watchers, crudely literal,
Stare and stare
Until the pair
Turn into moving stone.
The wart, the mole,
The crooked smile,
The known propensity to rile
In the moment's mythic whole
Are subsumed and are gone.

Arrival's here but is not here.
Mystery is what they dare.

They're at the door, the gauntlet's run
Of what a marriage can become.

Here's time seen through a dreaming-glass.
They are the dreamers. Let them pass.

No raucous glibness here where two
Walk as the one somnambulist.

Don't waken them until they do
In some sure, accidental room
Or public place where self-belief
Finds in the cup or ornament
Or careless phrase a cipher of
The death of hope and feels become
Harder realities and truth
Come naturally as loss of youth,
Touch hurt as final as a stone
And find their garrulous dreams go dumb
And be alone and catch the view
From that high edge we all come to,
Though some don't look, and like a leaf
That makes no sound but is a death
Fall from the boughs of their own faith
And come to, without telling, grief.

Living is the best and worst
Past the mind's demented peering,
Past the telling, past the hearing.
Here the institution ends and humanity begins.

III

Snap! Snap! You stand there
And you over here.
We'll have to do something
With that strand of hair.
If you make two rows
And adjust the bride's veil
(And explain that a flower girl
Should not pick her nose).
And now over here (avoid the dog crap).
Oh that's it, that's perfect, don't move now.
Snap! Snap!

The innocent sunlight is caught in a box.
While high up in its stillness some unnoticed flocks
Fly on into vast immemorial time.

But here on the ground the time-hunters are out
Moving in unison, hunting in packs,
Use the eye and the mouth and the sensitive snout
To capture the moment that's going to last,
Outwitting the future by keeping the past.

That's it, just like that. Get that dog, use that tree.
I got one when Harry was down on one knee.
Over here, no, don't smile, if you just turn your head.

The time-hounds are ravening, slaver, yap, yap
At the huge, crushing feet of inscrutable laws
And into stone ankles sink miniscule jaws
And don't hear the sound of their teeth breaking. Snap!

IV

'Wasn't she lovely?' 'He spoke well.'

The pleasure cages are alive
With screech and scream and yell.
Confinement can see vistas.
Laughter bounces like a ball.

In the bright room mouths are open to the fun
Like Gargantua with a pickle.
The drink's poured like a bottled sun.
The legs of Atlas buckle.

Death, the old bore, patrols his zoo
And prods the inmates with a stick.
They grab it from his hands and boo
And poke him with it back.

'No. She's the other cousin's wife. The one in blue.'
'Remember the carry-on. That's her man who . . .'

Gossip, history in its underwear,
Holds shells of strange seas to each ear.
The amazingness of what we do
Awes us again and teaches how

In any street an epic, any room
Strange stories never told, testaments dumb.
The richness overwhelms. A chance remark
Can touch new land, unload another ark.
Transactions of small change will sometimes yield
Coins of a minting you have never held.

Break any casual stone and find strange veins.
The colours blind. The anecdotes will range
Through wild geographies of spirit, form
Plain men with unknown flowers in their arms.
In each face new horizons, any day
An archaeology more rich than Troy

While, smiling from his private doom,
The groom's father's cousin, Brannigan,
Irish as Guinness, is practising
In some sealed chamber of his head
Where all his boyhood hopes lie dead
The song, drunk as a skunk, he sings to the wall of his room.

No woman softens what I feel
No child makes me a home.
I am a house of blazing lights
To which no one has come.
My father ploughed a bitter field
But I am ploughing stone.
I cuddle a great emptiness,
My dreams all live alone.

My dreams all live alone.
I'm married to the shovel now.
It's a heathenish affair.
A roster is my rosary,
Communion's bitter beer.
Give me a horse, I'll show you how—
It's tractors over here—
By Jesus, I could plough.

By Jesus, I could plough.
The field was by the sea.
There was a girl with haystack hair
Once sat across my knee.
I wonder if she's here the now,
I wonder if she'll marry me,
I wonder if she'll have my child.
Tomorrow, then, we'll see.

Hearts renew in the humus of old griefs
Brave pleasures that oppose demons of truth.

McPhater, local Munchausen,
Quaffs imagination's nectar in dark pints,
Constructor of fantastic architraves
Through which what never could have been is
As natural as sunlight on quartz lakes.

His tongue's a magic carpet. From his mouth
The smoke of burning cities issues.
He makes paupers of God's dreams. His manic hands
Fashion from air a planet.
He needs no seventh day, without pause makes
Atlantics swim with difficulty, legs
Cut off with rusty penknives (it was sore),
German lip-read through glasses from afar,
Saharas full of trees, cut down for logs
Because the nights were cold. Around him all
Cliff-hanging in a pelting storm of lies
Pass laughter like a rope, in case they fall.

Yet he has been real places, fought real war.
He knows the killing limits, where they are.
A daughter dead had viced his heart for years.
With pockets full of air he walked hard streets.
His body is a torture-box. Yet pain
Waters imagination with his tears.
Why should the actuality he meets
Where disasters big enough were never scarce
Evoke the cosmic vaudeville of his rant?

His gift perhaps is modesty, the thought
That life goes on by being not found out.
His lapwing patter shows us where he's not.

In the cleft between true grief, mock cataclysm
Unnoticed grows his casual heroism.

Around him words pace out their loneliness.
The nights are drawing in or out. If lamps,
It's amps, if golf it's to the turn in par.
Led on a leash of language, all
Our feelings take a quiet stroll,
A regular constitutional,
Once round the truth and back again.

'She lives alone now.' 'Never married, eh?'
Their words approach her and withdraw like deer.
She sits, forbidding pleasure to come near.
'She looks as if she's at a funeral.'

Her age has had three chambers. Yet the first
Was hardly private, crowded ante-room
Where eccentricity was uniform—
The tremor in the hands, the cataract,
Each action made to measure what you've lost.
Proudly apart, she put on loss of pride
Which held the second key, and stepped inside.

The place was worse, of course. For there she learned
Age wholly personal, never absolved by species.
She heard repeated what her life had said.
She found her age as something she had done.
Hands for so long capable to work
Others' sufferings into private bread
Held an intractable emptiness.
Eyes that refused to look at last had come
To sole perspective of a barren self.
Her chief art of rejection had found home.

The last place now is where she is. And there
Nothing seems possible unless a prayer
To the locum god, forgiveness for all,
That yet she learn forgiveness for one,
Compassion's iron hymen of despair
Be breached in her and somehow he may teach
Her mortal anguish to breed human speech
That it may live before forever dumb.
Certain it is that no one else can come,

Not even the children skating across the floor
On the thin ice of their parents' tolerance,
Thrown laughter balls, the young bucks of the beer,
Not the flashing of innumerable smiles
Like torches probing the darkness of her mood.

Uncle Davy, former navy,
Is communing with the past.
He finds an image, sudden, secret,
Golden, grieving, bright and painful,
At the bottom of a glass.

They were running, six-legged friendship,
Dreams in harness, fiercely straining

One was running lithely to a marriage where his own
Incompetence in hatred would condone
The slaughter of his hopes, a cunning pen
Where time was time and time and time again.
One was earning an oceanic thirst that would
Need such a slaking as could quench the sun
And sink despair forever. And for one
The horizon would be sudden.

The river wound with remorseless joy.
Fields can't abate their happy cunning.
Contemplating its own mystery, a world
Digested them at leisure and was sunning.
They were glad the way it was and they were running

To where beside the bar a group
Process experience, canned in jokes.

Ye heard aboot Benny the optimist?
A smile like a flooer oan a shroud.
He weers his ain blues
Like spit-poalisht shoes
An he pre-peys the tax oan aw bets.

The doactors said, Benny, it's lukkin bad.
They aw dee that hiv this disease.
Benny thoacht for a while
Pit oan a fresh smile
An said, Well, Ah'll no catch it twice.

So Frankenstein's monster meets this drunk Glaswegian . . .

See me. Ah'm comin' hame an' that. Ye know.
Distillery on legs. Knew Ah wis drunk.
Readin' the 'Warcry' in the pub. Wis so.
Sure sign. That stage Ah didny think. Ah *thunk.*
Ah'm walkin' careful, too. Ye know the way,
Wee asides to the universe an' that:
'Well, things'll have tae change. This'll no dae.
New rules.' Could see God reachin' for his hat.
Right on ma gemme. Walkin' that way ye've seen,
The world's a yard o' pavement an' no more.
Give it time to catch up from where ye've been
Or ye're off the edge. Oh here, Ah know the score.
Ah'm sayin' 'Oops' like, 'Oops-a-daisiltee.'
Stops, 'cause the head's still gaun like a wee champ.
'Those feet,' Ah tells God, 'don't belong to me.'
Smart enough tae give Einstein's heid a cramp.
An' Ah'm right enough. Each foot's a separate state.
Bloody enormous. Cow a boot for sure.
Brain startin' tae go at an awfy rate
Tryin' tae work things oot. Hard work's a hoor.

Feet's facin' me. Right ? Fair enough? No' mine.
'Excuse me, James,' Ah says. Message received.
No gonny mudge, Ah thinks. Very bad sign.
May have to leave his wife extra bereaved.
Starts tae look up. An' up. An' up. Aw shite!
Whit's this we've got? A tenement wi' feet?
Ah sees his face. Nae kiddin'. An erse wi' e'en.
Bolt stickin' oot his heid! Pathetic sight.
But Ah makes a quip: 'This isny Hallowe'en.'
Worser sense of humour ye'll never meet.

If fitba's sadness, big yin wins a cup.
Sensitive, me. Ah gets quite sad as well.
An' still Ah'm lookin' up an' up an' up.
'Western?' Ah says. 'Who sent ye oot like that?
Eejits,' Ah says. 'A liberty. Tae hell.
N H S couldny dress a bloody cat.' Sorry for the big yin, like.
Know whit Ah mean?
Christ, naebody should look like that. No squerr.
Sometimes drinkin', think over whit Ah've seen.
God's a big vandal. Takes me tae the ferr.
Says, 'Big yin, gonny pit the arms doon noo?
Hurtin' yer muscles that, son. Gonny relax?
That's better, son. Take yer brains aff the broo.'
Stertin' tae greet the big yin is. That's fac's.
'Son, son,' Ah says. 'Behave yerself. Come on!
Among freen's noo. Where dae ye want to go?
Ye fae Maryhill? Balornock? Where ye gaun?
The Briggs? The Drum? Poor bastart didny know.
He tried tae speak. Oh Christ. That wis a soon',
A kinna noise likely tae burst yer hert,
Bag o' kittens some'dy wis tryin' tae droon.
Ah says, 'Don't worry, son. Ah'll take yer pert.
Ye tried speech therapy, son? It could help, like.

Ye're gaun a bad road here—Saracen Street.
They'll likely take yer bolt oot for a bike.
Take ma advice, son. An' ye'll turn the feet.
Tell ye whit,' Ah says. 'The way ye're gaun,
Second-storey windaes. Be leanin' oot
Massagin' the heid wi' screwtaps. Tell ye, son,
That team doon there'll turn ye inside oot.
Ye're hame wi' me. Son, otherwise it' doom.

Jenny's all right. Her bark's worse than her bite.
Legs in the kitchen, heid in the back room,
Sleep like a top, no problem, son. All right?
Wee bevvy in the hoose. Quids in. Okay?'
Looked up. The pair big sowl had ran away.
Ah didny mean tae frighten him. Ye know?
There wis a likeable bit aboot him, tae.
Not a great talker certainly. That's true.
But Ah'd like tae meet the big yin any day.
Felt sorry for 'im. That's the story then.
Nae herm in the big fella really. Ah've seen men
Wid rust his bolt wi' fright. Know whit struck me?
How like he wis tae that big Tam McBride—
Wullie McBride's boay, moved tae Merrylee.
'Cept, is Tam's bolt no' on the ither side?

Margo, auntie of the bride,
Is talked to by a man who knew
The girl she used to be at school.
She was the one he wanted first,
Inventor of his body's thirst.
He made love to her endlessly
In a corner of his upstairs room
But in their countless assignations
He was the only one who came.
Seeing her next day in the class,
He'd look at her peculiarly
As if 'Your secret's safe with me.'

He inventories as he talks
The goitre chin, the tired eyes,
The upper arms that sag with flesh,
The accent, silver-plated tin,
And forgives her for not loving him.

(So love can be a clerk at last
Distraining on a bankrupt past.)

He smiles and mutters pleasantries
While in the dark behind his eyes
A small fifth-column plans its coup:

Your talk a loud parade,
Yourself a widow in a house it passes.

Forgive me tenacious affections
That worry the flesh of old times into bone.
And it's maybe something like love
To see that sheer girl
In your blunted postures.

My memory will be standing through cold nights,
A lonely nuisance that police can't shift,
Staring in moonlight at the window where
Your head aches in its curlers and your man,
Tupping and snoring, drowns in his own fat.

Tipping its hat as you take in the milk,
Its expression won't be utterly ironic.

I shall remember who you might have been.

But Margo is abstracted. She has seen
The bride and groom and through her like a spear
The image goes, impales her on a thought.
They are a couple now, she thinks. That word
Evokes in her misgivings. While she chats
Of where he's working now, somewhere within
A warning lecture takes shape to the bride.

'We think,' it says. 'Our feeling is,' it says.
Within that furtive, sterile, mutual gaze
No difference can survive. In its four eyes
The shock of truth is neutered to surprise.
As easy to strip to honesty that 'us'
As peel a jersey from an octopus.

It is a kind of monster. It will wrap
Itself around you slowly. It first clings
Then eats, both bait and trap.
Its two halves work in unison like jaws
Obeying their harsh unilateral laws,
Grinding the wild variety of things
To one vast universal ego-pap.

It must survive is all it thinks. Relax.
The danger is in envy. It would have
All selves expressed in its crude dual syntax.
Find no temptation in its furnished lair,
Its tame conclusions within easy reach,
The sated world-denying double stare,
Telekinesis of supportive speech.

Instead, returning to your wilderness,
Begin again with all. Exclusiveness
Is understanding's knackery. One
From concern with every other one is wrung.
Such 'love' is a well-mannered Genghis Khan
And pity it the deaths it lives among.

The bride has her own doubts, for she recalls,
Without willing it, the pub where he proposed
And memory provides her with an omen.

The place was lush, contained itself
In self-sufficient definition,
Irrigated with gentle conversations.
Piped music housed it like a plastic dome.
Small intimacies were arbours
Where the nice could iconize their niceness.
The barman leaned his ear
Quizzically to a shore of whispering shells.
He sweated discreetly. They were a mutual weather.

The door flung open. There a boy,
Say twelve, thirteen. His age, like where he came from,
Was his secret. Over his shoulder
A shiver of wintering stars.

The face a broken bit of stinging darkness
Daft with cold and gay with grimness.
He bellowed just, 'Ya durty bastards.'
The door chopped face and stars.
His laughter twinned another and their feet
Took a well of silence at two strides.

Just for a moment,
The darkness over everything like ash,
Grotesquely ornamental the conversation,
Baroque the jolly laughter, styles decadent,
The faces with their melting plastic smiles.
Just for a moment the weather broken
And a big night pelting silence on their hovel.

Then someone laughed,
Others shook sage, sophisticated heads
But she had thought all understood his message,
Where it suckled at the herds of roaming stars,
How his dare drew a part of them after it
Into the stinging cold
And the rest of them understood why it was waiting.

Rome was there to give barbarians a purpose.

'Don't volunteer for it,' the groom is told.
'The social square-drill.
The uniform was made for someone else.
Just watch him as he gets
The dandruff epaulettes
Of a general in the legions of the 'lost',
As he look towards his father and remembers

One day caught in a crystal
Lambent with warmth, sunflakes exploding round.
My father on the step at the back door
Throwing the ball.
Endless the rise and dip of the stuffed leather.

I dived, I jumped, I crouched, I sprang,
Fantastically agile,
Nijinsky in black sandshoes,
Making an epic out of every movement.

I was going to be a goalkeeper
And he talked.
Out of anonymous dole-queues
Like the smoke of a cigarette his drifting voice.
Coming from those recesses
He disappeared in, sitting at the fire
Staring through the pipe-smoke that he made.
Welling out of eyes he kept
For looking at the ceiling above his bed,
Head resting on clasped hands.
A thread of luminous dream.
For hours, for hours it seemed.

He said 'the college'.
He made a campus from his ignorance,
A place so bright with promise my eyes hurt.
He made long days for me,
Wide vista-mornings
Of learning and great talk and games and people.

He demanded very gently such a future,
Dressed in old trousers, open shirt.
My father could dream like Plato on a step.

Pitching through sunspots
I was raped with longing.

That night, of course, I cried. For I was nine.
Forever lying between me
And the living I would do.
Everything was only what I wanted.
My mother found me. Blunt wads
Of baffled meaning from my mouth.
And baffled still.

For the things I won't accomplish
For my father's college nobody has built
For the boy who secretly still boards in me.

For that warm, selfless woman,
For that hard, injured, baffled and brave man.

Beyond the ring of pleasure stands
A father with his children who
Are bored with things that adults do.
He must amuse them. He has found
In the foyer of this old hotel
(Which out of season has become
A private-enterprise old folks' home)
Something which holds their eyes entranced.
He improvises with their wonder
And tells a truth he doesn't know.

This strange machine is old now.
But with money they say it still works.
Only one patch of metal's been modernised—
The slot part, where you have to pay.

Isn't the workmanship marvellous?
Those figures look made out of skin.
There's the house and the family at home
The piano, the mother sat there.
Who are those three ragged children
Outside, with the door just ajar?
Why is only the maid at the window?
She could be their mother. An aunt?
Put a coin in and see where we are.

It's broken, you'd think. Heads are jerking
In communal seizure, all's discord—
The tuneless piano, the moaning
As if a real child were trapped there.
But wait, the machine knows its function.
Precision is coming to pass.
Don't crowd too eagerly forward
In case your breath clouds the glass.

The oldest boy's arm, see, it's moving:
A gesture like throwing a stone.
The maid shuts and opens the curtains.
In that time the children are gone.

Ah! The ground opens up to receive them.
Isn't this an amazing machine?
But is that a flaw? Looking closely,
You can see where their footprints have been.
But the ball that the small girl was holding
Is rolling. Now where will it go?
Look. It goes down through that grating.
So that's how the whole thing is done.

The lost ball's a trigger for something.
Look how the door has now closed.
All the lights have come on and bright flowers
Have popped up in that ornate vase
And all the fine people are nodding—
Don't they appear just divine?
See how their hands are all tapping,
See how their feet keep the time.
The maid has turned round and salaams.
They all seem transported by music.
Quite wonderful! Isn't that Brahms?

Too soon, though, it whirs into silence.
The people become again still.
Flowers vanish, the door has reopened—
See how the whole thing makes sense—
The children are back with the ball.

They say that it will work forever
Doing forever precisely the same
Just as long as the money keeps coming.
How we still love Victorian games!

Do you have another ten pence?

Auntie Belle gets up to sing
The sad songs that she so enjoys
In memory of husband, sons.
Her heart's a public thoroughfare
Of two-way traffic—pleasure, grief.
She lives one sheer belief.

Tell me the loass o' weans then
The world's weys that appal
The gully left that sheared a bairn,
Oorit chill an' the bus an' the broken fence
An' virus an' stane an' things unkent,
The infinite poallen o' daith.
Ah ken them, Ah ken them already
But that joay's a cannibal.
Ah ken an' like a mayflee
In a sunglint that gloams as it shines
Jist watch me dance in the meenit's glance
Daft as a wave fae a fullin' grave
An' be cuckoo wance again.

Her face is open and her smile's
A blank cheque to experience,
Her wink's defiance, her life one long
Jolly Country and Western song.

Much of his life was a drive-in movie.
The driving-mirror was the screen
Where his life was projected at angles
From which it was never seen.

No tears were shed for that passion,
No eyes beheld that drama
In the wonder of Mistavision
In the magic of Ignorama.

But his hair went grey at the temples
As his salesman's job went stale
And his eyes developed wrinkles
And his mouth a taste for gin
As his children couldn't stand him
As he went slowly bald
And his dreams were a joke
That he learned to tell
To keep the agony in
As his wife was a vale of tears
And nothing seemed right as his gut went sour
And it lasted thirty years.

Nobody understands the plot.
Nobody saw the end.
Nobody, least of all himself,
Saw the lorry come round the bend.

No critic gave an opinion
Of what we should think or feel
Or caught that subtle cloud, so far
From the mirror of the upturned car,
That took up the last reel.
Or the music that went on playing
Until a stranger turned it off—

Re-release of a song that when he began
Was playing again and again
And had given him hope wide as Cinemascope
And was a golden oldie then.

But he left two sons and a daughter
And a wildly embittered wife
Who knew at last she had been cast
In another B-picture of life.

No singer ever sang one song
While there remained some breath.
She calls it 'last performance'.
They hope she tells the truth.

I saw his last performance. The audience was small:
A nephew, a niece and a sister
And a great-niece and his wife.
The scene was a room that he wouldn't leave
Where they thought they had better call.
The theme was the end of a life.

He hadn't much to work with,
Only some chairs and a bed
And sunshine, a fading spotlight,
And the sureness that he would be dead.

He started slowly, uncertain,
As if he wasn't sure of his lines.
There was talk of the times and where we had been
And a roll-call of old friends.

But his confidence was growing
Honed on habitual strength.
His mind was an anti-fake machine
That worked, his anger a knife
And out through his smile and his vigorous style
Came seventy hard years of life.

The Depression had not been for nothing,
He still survived his War.
Show me the men who are more than him.
Please, take me where they are.

The room filled with a dying passion
That never became too much—
Such was the note he hit and held—
For his heart had perfect pitch.

He took the shy child in beside him,
He kidded her for an hour.
Laughing at his performance,
She bloomed on his death like a flower.

All right, so it was acting.
You can do better with breath
Than take each day in a personal way
And make a few faces at death?

A two-inch notice in the paper
Didn't matter much because
Till he went to the dead he winked and played
Human. And this is applause.

The voice has carried, pibroch-strange and shrill,
A wordless message to a private room
Where a resident is staring at the screen.
She never married, never will
And thinks of one it drove to kill.

She struck him. In the forging of the blow,
Black angels dancing on a needle-point,
A world of griefs came crowding to the light.
Their strident gibbering was fierce, as if
They knew their time at last for being born.
The ornamental eggs of rectitude
All cracked and there spilled out its vicious young,
Hates long denied, injustices endured
And truths time left to addle without hope.

It was all jab and tearing and they fed
Until he died and chaos became tame.
The orphans of her dreams were put to bed
And slept at once. The consequences came.

And she accepted them. They were surprised
How calm she was. She wondered if they knew
That passion is a force for order too,
One woman's love can blight for her the earth
And murder seem a way of giving birth.

She doesn't wish to share their folly,
Reaches across and turns the telly up.

Ha! Ha! Ha! I'm rich and famous.
Ha! Ha! Ha! All this is great.
I talk of marriage, Nostradamus,
Whether children should take drugs,
Love and death, the people's fate,
Philosophy, sea-going tugs.
It doesn't matter I can't tell
Elbow from arse about this blah
Because I've made a film as well.
Ha! Ha! Ha! Ha! Ha! Ha! Ha!

Har! Har! Har! I get the message.
I can laugh as loud as you,
Tell a story about massage.
Har! Har! Har! Now I tell two.
Har! Har! Bought this dress from Dior,
Sit beside me and drop dead.
I'm so lovely they won't wonder
Where the hell I bought my head.
You've no chance, you're with a big star.
Har! Har! Har! Har! Har! Har! Har!

He! He! He! We're all so funny
I'm going to wet myself tonight.
No wonder we get so much money
For being beautiful and bright.
He! He! He! There's just one problem:
We can't see this gorgeous show.
I only hope my stupid mother
Has it on the video.
Sh! I'm talking world to thee.
He! He! He! ME! ME! ME! ME!

But loud as the chat-show guests can laugh
She cannot quite forget those dreams
That Romeoed up the rone-pipe of her parents' council house.

She wonders what it's like to be a bride.
The bride is wondering, too. She and the groom
Can hear the voices of the guests recede.
The night will funnel to a final room.

Endless labyrinthine teens
I wandered in, each corridor
Foetid with failure. Who is this?
Theseus or the Minotaur?

The night will funnel to a final room.
Imagination, close the door.
Miracles may yet take place,
Incantations summon grace.
May they find our good but petty
Wishes like well meant confetti
Sequin their discarded clothes.

V

Here the population's two.
No bus or train comes this far out.
The guests are gone, the public gestures hang,
Creak in the wardrobe waiting to be worn.
Here's where our bodies talk for us.

One is the lock and one the key.
There is a word we have to say.

The word is love. It does not mean
Anything we can understand.

The door is we. It opens where
None of us has been before.

It shuts behind us as we pass.
The only profit is in loss.

The word is love. The door is we.
One is the lock and one the key.

Touch, occult language we relearn.
Touch, necromancer. Skin will burn.
Mole, mouths, along your hunger's labyrinth.

Touch. This is a jaw, this is a knee,
A belly, a breast, a billow of thigh,
This is the braille of the blinded self.

Touch. Heal the scars that our clothes have left.

Touch me, touch you, touch and not know
Where each body ends, where each begins,
The edges melt, contours dissolve,
Selfhood is breaking, the weltering wins.

Flesh is the ocean where lust has grown fins.

Touch. Pores bloom to orchids.

Touch. Here's a snuffle, a mewing of cats,
A sword out of flesh, a flower out of the hair,
A sun in the hands, a meadow of fire,
Here are strange thoughts that glow in the dark
And burn to the bone. And you will have been
The metamorphoses of manifold skin.

Processions of strange painted selves,
Mind that ignites, flesh that has helves
Where secret images are borne
From where the blind lips can divine
The places of the hidden wells
Of body to the only source.

Madness assuming divinity,
The rods spurts life, the chalice fills.

Feast of the earthly trinity,
The bush burns where thighs meet.

Altered we lie in altered place
And wonder where is this new-formed face,
This river-veined abandoned hand.

In new-found-recently-seismic-land.

What are these blood-sounds fading now,
The whinny and the muted low,
The grunting and the dying bark?

The animals that missed the ark.

Now be patient. Talk awhile
To eyes that grow new sight, the smile
That floats on lust's spent eddies.

Beware, beware. See where we are.
Passion grows a secret mouth
That came to eat the world.

Ceremony is the word.
If we would storm the darkest god
He'll husk us with his fire.

There is a time to touch the hair
And name in gestures of quiet care
The children of our passion,

A time to hold with no intent
But to express a mutual want
That promises a future,

A second coming of sweet sadness,
The gentle fit that follows madness
And knows that they are kin.

These rites, too, the god ordains
That lovers may be also friends
And shield themselves from him.

We learn from pleated bodies now the weaving of the one.
Surely no parting's possible, or if it came
Would char the world in one last flame,
Be the last leaf, last word to speak.
Surely such parting were unique.

All partings are the one.
No noted oddness of the leaves,
Rain in its whispered complicity,
Light that bends to our mood and grieves,
No heart-tearing cry, no whim-chosen star
Will alter the commonplace we are.
Each parting must do what others have done,
Be share of the void we fill with our heart.
Partings are one.

And does the end of loving come
When two who have believed they can be one
Discover they are two and on a narrow ledge
And just one foothold there and death is sheer?
And is that where grows jealousy's wild fear?

We will be that as well, each other's body's beauty's pander.
Mind is a wanton for thought,
Leches with misconceptions as it trusts.
Starved by absence, love eats what is not
When nothing else is there.

From one missed phone-call
We will quickly make a wilderness of fears to wander in,
Roar through it like a baptist to announce
The coming of a terrible false god
And be amazed to find the world goes on.
We will regret that nothing is destroyed.

In eyes that see another, we will see
Half-open doors, behind them treacheries
We never will unfold, swift lecheries
Who part just as they meet
So that we see but cannot know we've seen.

A hesitance in speech, a foreign smile
Will send our hunger for the truth out
Like a hunting Hopi, mile on mile.

Here's a nice jungle: glades of trust
Disturbed by parakeets of lust,
Pools of deceptive calm where need
Bathes among crocodiles of greed.

It could not have been other. Love abjures
All glamour, strips itself to the raw pores
And that is dangerous. We who adhere
In love's sweat to each other learn the art
Of bringing skin off with us as we part.

Love may lie naked but it learns to keep
Its arts about it, even in its sleep—
Always to hand the knife beneath the pillow,
Glass that was ground down from an old abuse,
Poison of hurt phialled for a later use.

And where is safety for us now?

The word has been given. The word is all.
The word is empty. It will fill
With who believe the word is all.

It is the word we try to keep.
Lie down in it and we will sleep.

And so adrift in unknown selves we lie
Abandoned to dark plucks of circumstance,
Not knowing what will come or what we'll do
Or where the tides of sleep will wash us and
Shy from the sculling shapes that feed on mind,
Feel every certainty drift out of reach
And sigh and hold each other, tryst with touch
To share what is not shareable, and know
The jerking terror of time's undertow
And madly try to dream ourselves a beach.

In madness there endures one sanity:
The courage of our shared humanity.

We wake now in another day.
And see ourselves and can't believe
That was the bottomless shaft where all
Who love must hang but must not fall.

The last gift is self-doubt by which
We walk the fire and are not scorched.

'I love you, I need —' the one will say.
'I need you, I love —' the other. We'll see.

'You beauty!' the harpooner said to the whale
Then took it apart from the head to the tail.

This is the coming back to land
From where we could not go. The sounds
Of other lives define the day.
Wild shapes resolve to furniture,
The ocean laps and finds a bay.